**NO LONGER PROPERTY OF
GLENDALE LIBRARY ARTS
& CULTURE DEPT.**

P9-DTF-617

AMERICAN SHORTHAIR CATS

by Mari Schuh

AMICUS HIGH INTEREST • AMICUS INK

j 636.822 SCH

Amicus High Interest and Amicus Ink are imprints of Amicus
P.O. Box 1329, Mankato, MN 56002
www.amicuspublishing.us

Copyright © 2017 Amicus. International copyright reserved in all
countries. No part of this book may be reproduced in any form without
written permission from the publisher.

Library of Congress Cataloging-in-Publication Data
Schuh, Mari C., 1975- author.
American shorthair cats / by Mari Schuh.
    pages cm. -- (Favorite cat breeds)
Audience: K to grade 3.
Summary: "A photo-illustrated book for early readers about American
Shorthair cats. Describes the cat's unique features, great hunting skills,
social behaviors, and how they act as pets"-- Provided by publisher.
Includes bibliographical references and index.
ISBN 978-1-60753-967-4 (library binding)
ISBN 978-1-68152-096-4 (pbk.)
ISBN 978-1-68151-001-9 (ebook)
1. American shorthair cat--Juvenile literature. 2. Cat breeds--Juvenile
literature. I. Title.
SF449.A45S38 2017
636.8'22--dc23
                          2015028751

Photo Credits: small1/Shutterstock cover; VladislavStarozhilov/iStock
2; Tumpsk/Shutterstock 4-5; libusca/Getty Images 6; flyfloor/iStock 6;
Ryuichi Miyazaki/Getty 9; jbhann/iStock 10; Brian Kimball/Kimball Stock
13; Creativ Studio Heinemann/imageBROKER/Corbis 14-15; Renata
Apanaviciene/Shutterstock 17; chanon sawangmek/Shutterstock 18-19;
Jirawat Chungviwatanant/Dreamstime 21; VladislavStarozhilov/iStock 22

Editor: Wendy Dieker
Designer: Tracy Myers
Photo Researcher: Derek Brown

Printed in the United States of America.

HC 10 9 8 7 6 5 4 3 2 1
PB 10 9 8 7 6 5 4 3 2 1

For Sam, Sadie, and Sasha—MS

TABLE OF CONTENTS

RELAXED CATS

A relaxed cat sits in a window. The cat's body is **stocky**. This cat is strong. Its big, round eyes watch birds outside. The cat is an American Shorthair.

HISTORY

Shorthair cats came to North America with early settlers. They traveled on ships from Europe. The cats caught mice and rats on the ships. These Shorthairs became good working cats in America.

Like a Wild Cat?

American Shorthairs are still good hunters. Like wild cats, they sneak up on prey. They pounce. They catch small animals.

STRONG AND POWERFUL

American Shorthairs are powerful cats. They have a muscular body. They are good climbers. Their strong legs help them jump.

MANY COLORS

American Shorthairs have short, thick fur. It feels **stiff**. These cats can be more than 80 colors and patterns. A silver **tabby** pattern is common.

Like a Wild Cat?

Some Shorthairs have stripes. An orange tabby looks a little like a small tiger.

SWEET FACES

An American Shorthair has a sweet face. It has round, wide-set eyes. It has a big head and full cheeks. People think they are cute.

KITTENS

American Shorthairs often have four kittens at a time. Kittens are born with their eyes closed. After about 10 days, they open their eyes. The mothers are patient with their kittens.

Fun Fact
How old do these cats get? They can live for 20 years!

CALM YET PLAYFUL

American Shorthair cats **adapt** to their homes. They are calm in quiet homes. They can be playful, too. They are active in busy homes.

Fun Fact
American Shorthairs can have a silent meow. Sometimes, they open their mouths, but do not make a sound.

ON THEIR OWN

American Shorthairs do not beg for **attention**. They can play games by themselves. These cats do not need to be busy. They often like to relax.

FRIENDLY PETS

American Shorthairs are **social** cats. They are friendly. Some will sit on their owner's lap. They like to be with other pets and kids. American Shorthair cats are sweet, beautiful pets.

HOW DO YOU KNOW IT'S AN AMERICAN SHORTHAIR?

big head and full cheeks

big, round, wide-set eyes

strong, stocky body

short, thick coat

round paws with heavy pads

WORDS TO KNOW

adapt - to change for a different situation

attention - playing and being with someone or something

social - enjoys being with a group of people or animals

stiff - hard and not easily bent

stocky - having a big, heavy body

tabby - a striped coat

LEARN MORE

Books

Holland, Gini. *American Shorthairs*. Cats Are Cool. New York: PowerKids Press, 2014.

Leaf, Christina. *American Shorthairs*. Cool Cats. Minneapolis: Bellwether Media, 2016.

Websites

Cat Fanciers' Association: For Kids
http://kids.cfa.org/index.html

CATS Protection: All About Cats
http://www.cats.org.uk//cats-for-kids/about-cats/

INDEX

Every effort has been made to ensure that these websites are appropriate for children. However, because of the nature of the Internet, it is impossible to guarantee that these sites will remain active indefinitely or that their contents will not be altered.